?R/   ⋎

Term-time opening hours·

dealing with
SUBSTANCE ABUSE

Yvette Solomon

John Coleman

Wayland

Bullying

Eating Disorders

Relationships

Substance Abuse

Death

Family Break-up

Book editor: Louise Woods

Series editor: Deb Elliott

Book design: Helen White

First published in 1995

by Wayland (Publishers) Ltd

61 Western Road, Hove,

East Sussex BN3 1JD

British Library Cataloguing in Publication

Data

Solomon, Yvette

Substance Abuse. - (Dealing With Series)

I. Title II. Coleman, John III. Series

362.29

ISBN 0 7502 0990 9

Typeset by White Design

Printed and bound by Canale in Turin, Italy

All of the people who appear in the
photographs in this book are models.

Acknowledgements
The publishers would like to thank the following for allowing
their photographs to be reproduced in this book: Simon
Annand 20; APM 5, 21, 34; Camera Press 7 (Jan
Badenhurst); Chapel Studios 32; Sally and Richard
Greenhill 16, 18, 25, 29, 31; David Hoffman 8, 12, 38, 39;
Impact 9 and 23 (Simon Shepheard), 10, 13 (Paul Lowe),
19 (Bruce Stephens), 27 (Mark Cator); Mary Evans Picture
Library 4; Reflections 15, 26, 35, 37, 42, 43; Science Photo
Library 17; Tony Stone Worldwide 24, 40. Artwork on page
21 is by John Yates.

Contents

Drugs
and why we use them

Part of the problem in dealing with drugs lies in the fact that it's difficult to say exactly what drugs are. We might say that a drug is something that changes people's behaviour, or the way in which they see the world, but this would also be true of a number of things which we would not call drugs – the chemicals which are naturally present in our bodies and brains, for instance, or some foods that we eat, like sugar, 'E' number food colourings or preservatives, or oranges for migraine sufferers. Although drugs as we understand them do have an effect on what people say, do and think, they do not all do so in the same way and different group names for drugs – depressants, stimulants and hallucinogens – reflect this fact.

▼ **Drugs have been around for many years, in all walks of life.**

Drugs past and present

It is true to say that drugs play an important part in all sections of our society today, but it is not true to say that they are more important today than they were in the past. It is interesting that many drugs which are illegal and frowned on today were thought of

very differently even in the recent past. Sherlock Holmes' use of cocaine, or the Victorian poet Coleridge's use of opium were not thought of as particularly 'wrong' at the time. More recently still, amphetamines were given to World War II soldiers in combat, have been used by sportsmen and women to improve performance, and are used by lorry drivers and swotting students to keep awake for long periods. In the 1950s and 60s amphetamines were widely prescribed for depression and to suppress appetite in people who wanted to slim. Now they are

▲ **Drugs are found in many of the everyday things we eat and drink.**

considered to be dangerous drugs and are very rarely prescribed. Similarly opium was once available over the counter, and opiates and other powerful drugs have been widely used in children's cough medicines and sleeping aids. Minor tranquillizers, although known to be addictive, are still today the most widely prescribed drugs in Britain, with over 20 million prescriptions a year. Twice as many women as men use them, and many are dependent to some extent. This prescribed use is socially acceptable, but the illegal use of tranquillizers is not.

Alcohol and nicotine as drugs

People have used alcohol for centuries, and it has been considered an acceptable drug for most of that time, except in certain societies or religious groups. But although alcohol is not usually described as a drug, it is, in fact, the most widely-used member of the depressant family of drugs. In the same way, we rarely think of a cigarette as containing a drug, even though we know that nicotine is highly addictive and has definite effects, such as calming you down and taking away your appetite. Probably because the use of alcohol and nicotine is legal in this country, we tend to see drinking and smoking as social habits, not as 'using drugs'.

The 'drug culture'

What really tends to make a difference to how we see drugs and drug use is the social acceptability of drugs. The large number of illegal drugs around today means that there is a kind of 'drug culture' which young people come into contact with. An important part of this culture is its illegality: for the few young people who get deeply involved in illegal drugs, the chances are they will also become involved in crime as adults.

Although the use of illegal drugs is on the increase, and around one in five secondary school pupils will have used them at some time, for most young people that is all. They may have tried a drug once or only occasionally but hardly ever become dependent. Very few young people will use illegal drugs on a daily basis, although slightly more will use alcohol or cigarettes. Teenagers are very unlikely to use 'hard' drugs such as cocaine, crack or heroin, and they are also unlikely to inject drugs. Their drug use tends to be social – at discos, parties and so on – and they tend to use drugs like cannabis, amphetamines and ecstasy. Many people stay with this 'recreational' use of illegal drugs and alcohol, keeping their drug use in control.

Why young people use drugs

There are a number of reasons why young people choose to use drugs. An obvious one is that it makes you feel more adult, as using drugs is something which older teenagers and adults do. If you don't have any experience of drugs or alcohol, then it seems

that you are missing out on part of being an adult. And everyone gets to a point where they are fed up with being young and not being taken seriously. Another reason young people experiment with drugs is that they have very little power over their own lives – they always have to do what adults say, and this is one way to feel independent. One of the best things about being an adult is being in control of your own life. But this also means being in control of drugs and alcohol, means recognizing your own limits and stopping when you've had enough.

▲ **Alcohol and cigarettes are more socially acceptable as they are not illegal.**

Another idea is that using drugs is a way of rebelling against parents or teachers or society in general. This is likely to be because the rules set down by adults (or, in the case of drugs, the law itself) may seem pointless or just made to please them. While this may be the case, you have to think about whether your actions really do affect adults in the way you want, and whether what you are doing is what you really want to do. It's also worth thinking about whether your parents really do disagree with you and your views about what the law should be, or whether they are just trying to protect you from getting into trouble.

Another reason why you might want to use drugs is simply to have a good time and to find out what a drug is like. There's no doubt about it – alcohol and many drugs make you feel good. They may make you feel relaxed and happy, they may even make you see the world in new and interesting ways. The question here is: 'When does feeling good become feeling bad, both in the short and the long term?' You have to learn to recognize the changeover point and make a decision for yourself which is realistic in terms of what you want out of life.

Closely linked to 'having a good time' is 'blotting out bad feelings'.

◀ **Many young people first try drugs just to find out what they do.**

▲ **Others use them as an escape from their problems.**

There's a narrow line dividing these two, and you have to decide whether you're just enjoying yourself taking the occasional drug for fun or whether you're simply numbing your mind because you can't cope with life for whatever reason. Quite a few young people are in this situation, maybe because things are really bad at home, or because they are out of work or homeless, or because they are mentally ill or depressed. If you're in this situation, you need to seriously consider getting help.

Finally, many young people use drugs simply because their friends do and because they feel pressurised into doing the same. Everyone, including adults, wants to fit in with others and not stick out like a sore thumb or at least be accepted for being different. It's very easy to get labelled as odd because you don't do the same things as other people. Hanging on to what you want to do and what you feel safe and happy doing is very difficult. But staying in control and handling pressure means you are growing up.

What drugs are and what they do

Drugs are divided into three main groups: depressants, stimulants and hallucinogens. These have different short term and long term effects.

Depressants
Depressants are a group of drugs which generally slow down the brain and the nerves which control our bodies.

Alcohol
The most often used depressant drug is ethyl alcohol, which is made from fermenting fruit, vegetables or grains. Beer is 1 part alcohol to 20 parts water and wine is 2-4 parts of alcohol to 20 parts water. Spirits, such as whisky, vodka, gin and brandy are almost half alcohol. Alcohol can be measured in units, which people use to see if they're safe to drive or to see if they are drinking too much. All the following drinks have one unit of alcohol:
**half a pint of ordinary beer
a single measure of spirits
(e.g. whisky, vodka, brandy)
one glass of wine
one small sherry
one measure of martini
(a normal measure of martini
is the same as two measures
of spirits)**

Although in the very short term it *appears* to act as a stimulant – alcohol makes people more talkative and less shy – this is due to a general slowing down effect. At the same time as making you feel more relaxed, the alcohol is actually slowing down the working of your brain. If you carry on, you eventually become unconscious. This slowing down makes people less alert when driving, for instance, and generally less careful and in control, both mentally and physically. Not everyone reacts to alcohol in the same way, though. How affected you are depends on how much alcohol is in your blood supply, and this depends on your size and weight, your sex, and how fast you drink. In a tall person blood simply has further to go, so that the amount going to any part of the body will be less than the same amount going to any part of a small person's body. Women usually have more fat and less water in their bodies than men, which means that the level of alcohol in their blood will be higher than men's after drinking the same amount of alcohol, because fatty tissue has a poor blood supply. Alcohol is broken down by the liver, but only slowly, so if you drink fast, the level of alcohol in the blood will rise as your liver can't cope with the 'backlog'. Your surroundings and mood also make a difference to the effect that alcohol has on you. If you are at home with family or at a party with friends, you may find a good mood getting better after a few drinks. But if you are feeling aggressive when you start to drink, you will probably get more so.

Alcohol drunk in large quantities for a long period of time can do real damage to the body in the form of cirrhosis of the liver, ulcers, heart disease and brain damage. You can become mentally and physically dependent on alcohol, and if you give up drinking suddenly you may get symptoms like sweating, anxiety, trembling, hallucinations and delusions.

Heroin and other opiates
Heroin, also known as 'smack', 'junk', 'H', and 'skag', usually appears as a white powder and is made from the opium poppy. Other opiates come in the form of pink or white tablets.

In the short term, heroin, morphine and opium make you feel relaxed, dreamy and separate from the rest of the world. Your breathing and heart rate slow down. But taking too much heroin can cause unconsciousness and even death from breathing failure. Death can

also be caused by an accidental overdose, often of heroin that is unusually pure.

In the longer term, if you use opiates regularly, your body is likely to become very used to the drug, so that a higher dose is needed to get the same effects. You are likely to become mentally dependent and sometimes physically dependent on it. One result of this is that if you suddenly stop using the drug, you may feel very ill, as if you have bad 'flu'. But withdrawal symptoms are not always as awful as people think – research shows that how bad they are depends on how much and how long you

have been using the drug, and even on where you are and what is happening around you.

Like many other drugs, heroin is not usually sold in its pure form, but is mixed with other substances to make it go further and make more money for the seller. Together with dirty or infected needles, these impure drugs can cause real damage to health when they are injected.

▼ **All these items form part of the ritual of taking heroin. This ritual can be addictive in itself.**

Barbiturates and tranquillizers

Barbiturates, known also as 'barbs', 'downer', 'blues' and 'reds', and tranquillizers, or 'tranx' include sedatives and sleeping pills, and are often sold as coloured capsules or prescribed as Valium, Librium, Atavan or Mogadon pills.

Barbiturates can have the same effects as alcohol in the short term, making you feel relaxed and happy, but they can also make you feel confused and depressed. They can be very dangerous as accidental overdosing is easy to do. The danger is even greater if they are mixed with alcohol, when they can lead to blackouts and possibly death. Tranquillizers slow you down mentally, too, but do not make you feel sleepy as barbiturates do. But taking too many tranquillizers, especially with alcohol or barbiturates, is highly dangerous.

Both barbiturates and tranquillizers can quickly become mentally and physically addictive. They can also make you seriously ill, causing bronchitis and pneumonia. These risks are greater when the drug is injected. Coming off barbiturates suddenly can be dangerous and can kill. Withdrawal from tranquillizers is not so bad, but symptoms of sleeplessness, anxiety and sickness may take several months

to stop if you have taken these drugs for a long time.

Stimulants
Stimulants speed up the activity of the brain and nervous system, making people feel energetic and alert.

Amphetamines
Also known as 'speed', 'uppers', 'sulphate', 'sulph' and 'whizz', amphetamines are man-made

▲ **Stimulants give you energy to begin with.**

chemicals sold as powders, pills or capsules. To begin with, amphetamines make you feel energetic, confident and happy. They also take away your appetite. But taking too much can make you feel panicky and paranoid, and if you keep on taking them you can become tetchy and anxious.

In the long term, in order to keep getting the pleasant effects from amphetamines, you have to increase the dose. Using them more and more leads to side effects such as itchiness, loss of appetite, disturbed sleep, anxiety and paranoia. There can be long term damage to your health, like heart failure or a stroke, and your mental health may suffer. Stopping is unpleasant – you may feel depressed and tired for some time, but these symptoms are not dangerous in themselves, although some people may become suicidal.

Cocaine and crack
Cocaine, also known as 'coke' and 'snow', is a white powder made from the cocoa shrub. It is usually sniffed, but can be injected. Crack, or 'freebase', is a purer form of cocaine which looks like a small crystal, and can be smoked.

Short term effects of crack and cocaine are very similar to those of amphetamines – feelings of excitement and alertness. These effects last for a far shorter time, though: 20 – 30 minutes for cocaine, and even less for crack, compared to 3 – 4 hours for a single dose of amphetamines. Taking too much can produce the same bad effects – anxiety and paranoia, and hallucinations. It is possible, although rare, to die from breathing failure or heart attack.

The effects of cocaine and crack can be so pleasant that it is easy to develop mental dependence, or addiction. Stopping isn't awful, but it makes you feel tired and depressed, so the urge to keep using these drugs is strong. Snorting cocaine for a very long time eventually does lasting damage to your nose.

Ecstasy
Also called 'white doves', 'disco burgers' and 'New Yorkers', Ecstasy is made from amphetamines, and is sold as a white, pink, brown, or yellow tablet, or as coloured capsules.

Ecstasy has a calming effect, and makes you notice sounds and colour more than usual. Taking too much can make you feel anxious and confused, and keeping on taking it can make you sleepless and paranoid.

Although Ecstasy does not make you physically dependent, your body gets used to it and you need more to get the same effect. Like amphetamines, if Ecstasy is used heavily, it increases the risk of a heart attack or mental illness in some people.

Hallucinogens
This group of drugs affects how you see the world, largely by distorting reality in some way, or by producing hallucinations.

LSD
Commonly known as 'acid', LSD is a man-made white powder, usually put into pills or capsules, sugar lumps or blotting paper.

To some extent, the short term effects depend on how you are feeling at the time, and whether you are in friendly or unfriendly surroundings. You may feel positive effects like noticing sounds or colour more than usual. You may also feel intense happiness and a general sense of joy and beauty. A bad trip can give you feelings of depression and panic.

LSD is not addictive in any way, and is not known to cause any damage to health, although it is just possible that using it might lead to some form of mental illness.

Magic mushrooms
These are mushrooms which contain the chemical psilocybin. There are about twelve kinds of these mushrooms, which grow wild in many parts of the country.

▶ **LSD can leave you feeling isolated and in a panic.**

Eating magic mushrooms produces similar effects to LSD, although perhaps these effects are not quite as strong. A short term danger is the risk of making a mistake and eating a poisonous mushroom instead. As with LSD, there are no known long term effects from eating magic mushrooms.

◀ **Not only glues are used for sniffing – aerosol sprays are also very common.**

Other drugs
Some drugs do not fit into any of the other groups.

Cannabis
Made from the plant cannabis sativa, cannabis (or 'dope', 'blow', 'grass', 'hash', 'shit', 'draw', 'wacky backy' amongst other names), usually comes in the form of resin, a dark brown solid mass which is crumbled and smoked with tobacco.

Cannabis has both depressant and slightly hallucinogenic effects in the short term. Low doses make you feel happy, relaxed and talkative. Higher doses can distort your vision and make you feel anxious and depressed. Many people have used cannabis over a very long period of time with no obvious damage to mind or body, and without moving on to harder drugs like heroin. The main obvious danger is doing yourself physical damage such as getting bronchitis or lung cancer from constantly inhaling smoke.

Glue-sniffing and solvents
Many substances are inhaled, including aerosol sprays (like hairsprays), lighter fuel, certain glues, dry-cleaning fluids, paint and paint thinners, correcting fluids and petrol.

Inhaling these substances has anaesthetic, hallucinogenic and sedative effects, but if you inhale deeply or for a long time you can lose control and consciousness. You recover quickly from this, although you might have a slight hangover. Short term dangers include accidents if you lose consciousness in a dangerous place, suffocation if you put a plastic bag over your head and, occasionally, heart failure.

If you keep on sniffing over a long period of time, you will probably become tired, depressed and trembly. You may lose weight and find it difficult to concentrate. These symptoms all stop when you stop sniffing. Long term sniffing may cause permanent damage to your brain, liver or kidneys.

Nicotine
This drug is found in the leaves of the tobacco plant. Nicotine is often described as a stimulant, but it can also have sedative effects. Smoking a cigarette may make you feel immediately relaxed and mildly stimulated, but only for a short time. You quickly get to the point when you are smoking several cigarettes a day to keep the effect going.

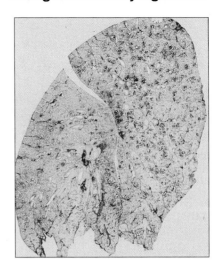

A lung blackened by cigarettes.

The long term effects of cigarettes are well known. Every year, at least 100,000 people in the UK die before they should because they smoke cigarettes. Constantly inhaling tobacco smoke can cause heart disease, blood clots, lung infections, strokes and bronchitis. A rough calculation is to say that each cigarette shortens the life of a regular smoker by five and a half minutes. If you smoke when you are pregnant, you are likely to have a small or premature baby and you may even lose the baby just before it is born. But giving up smoking suddenly can make you feel restless and depressed.

Group work activity
Devise an alcohol, smoking and drugs awareness programme for your school. What is your message? How can you get it across? Carry out a survey to measure its effectiveness.

Who's in control?

Whatever age they are, most people want to fit in with the particular group they belong to, whether they're into train spotting or acid house. But when you're a teenager, the need to fit in is perhaps stronger than at any other time. Strangely enough, one reason why this might be is that at this point in your life you are going through a huge number of changes – your body is changing, your relationships with your parents are changing, you are developing sexual relationships and what happens at school is more important than before. Faced with all this, many teenagers need an anchor point in terms of knowing who and what they are, and as friends play a bigger part in your life than they ever did before, they become part of that anchor. As you experiment with different selves, you need someone to tell you that you've got it right.

Peer pressure

The problem is, of course, that what friends think can become so important that you end up doing things you don't want to do. This is either because you're actually being pressurized into it by others, or because you're pressurizing yourself – like feeling that you must drink as much as your friends or take the same drug that everyone else is taking. There's no easy solution to this situation, but if you are doing something that you don't really want to do, you might think about the following points:

1. Where is the pressure coming from? Is it other people or is it really you yourself? If it's you, you need to think through your motives – are you showing off to a possible future girlfriend or boyfriend? Are you doing it to be accepted by a group? It's worth working out why you feel you must do something, and deciding whether it's worth it. Remember, too, that if you are pressurizing yourself, you may also be pressurizing others without realizing it – maybe the person you fancy is trying to keep up with *you*. Don't use the group as an excuse – the choice at the end of the day is yours.

▶ **Life can be difficult if you don't have a group of friends to join in with.**

▲ **Sometimes you may need to talk to someone outside your group of friends.**

2. Nobody has the right to make you do anything you don't want to do. If they are really forcing you, you need to think about whether you should be going around with them or whether you should drop them as friends. Maybe you need to get someone else's help – a sympathetic teacher, relative or the parent of one of your friends, or possibly someone else in your group of friends who may be in the same situation.

3. If you are being pressurized, say so. Some people may not realize that this is what they're doing, but if they do, having the whole thing out will force them to say why they think you should join in. Their arguments will probably sound pretty pathetic. Your argument is that everyone can and should decide for themselves what they do with their minds and bodies.

4. Being different doesn't necessarily mean that you can't be part of a group, or that your friends will reject you. But if they can't accept you the way you are – and that may include admitting that yes, you *are* scared to death of sniffing hairspray with a plastic bag over your head – that's their problem.

Advertising and the media

Part of the problem is that we are surrounded by images of how we should be in films, books, music, TV programmes and advertising. Young people who are trying to work out what kind of person they are will be particularly influenced by these images, without realizing that often they aren't realistic. Drug addiction and alcoholism is often made to look romantic in the music press, for instance, whereas in reality it may mean sickness and loneliness. More subtle images in films and TV programmes show 'tough guys' as smokers and fashionable

young people as drug takers. Smoking and drinking is made to look sophisticated by clever advertising, and is often associated with a particular kind of lifestyle that many of us would want – wining and dining in a smart restaurant, or being with well-dressed friends on a sunny beach. In fact, smoking and drinking is more likely to land you in the doctor's waiting room, whereas lounging around on a Caribbean beach simply requires a lot of money.

Drinking and smoking for women

As we have already seen, women are more affected by alcohol than men. It takes effect more quickly and this effect lasts longer, partly because women are usually smaller than men and partly because women's bodies have more fat and less water than men's. This means that the alcohol is more concentrated and stays in the body longer. It also has more effect if you drink a few days before your period starts or

before you ovulate (about two weeks before your period starts). If you are on the pill, alcohol is absorbed into the bloodstream more slowly and stays in the body longer, which means that you may drink faster at first because you will not feel the effects so quickly.

What all this adds up to is that girls need to be more careful than boys about how much they drink – the recommended limit for men is 21 units a week and only 14 for women. But the evidence is that

◄ **Glamorous lifestyles can often mask unhappiness.**

▲ **To stay healthy, women should drink less alcohol per week than men.**

girls go over their limit more often than boys do and so are more at risk from alcohol-related illnesses. One reason why this might be is that girls are more likely to go to pubs with older boys who have more money and are more used to drinking. Girls may feel pressurized in this situation to drink more than they want to so as to look sophisticated and to keep the relationship going.

Women are also a target for the tobacco advertising industry. Advertisers realised a long time ago that girls and women are easy prey when it comes to telling them what they should look like and how they should act. Women are far more likely than men to worry about their appearance and to want to change it to please someone else. As long ago as the 1930s, Lucky Strike cigarettes were advertised as helping women to lose weight with the caption 'Reach for a Lucky instead of a sweet'. More recently, adverts aimed at women show beautiful, slim, fashionable women posing with long, thin cigarettes. The message is that smoking is sophisticated and attractive, and that it's the thing to do if you're a liberated woman. If you think about it, nothing could be further from the truth.

Not losing control

Losing control is not inevitable – look at all the people who drink

alcohol only when they want to and are able to turn down another drink because they've had enough, because they're driving, or simply because they've been out quite a lot lately and want to have an alcohol-free day for their health's sake. The same goes for many of the illegal drugs – it's possible to control your drug use so that it doesn't ruin your life or anybody else's. Studies of drug users in Britain, Holland and the USA found that quite a few people had jobs and looked after families but nevertheless had used drugs for a long time. In Holland, regular drug users actually used less than when they first started – they weren't on a pathway to addiction.

What all this means is that you don't have to lose control, either by using a drug you'd prefer not to use, or by becoming hopelessly addicted. You need to be honest with yourself about your motives and learn to recognize the pressures on you from both inside and outside, and how they work. You also need to be able to tell when you've got a problem.

Group work activity

Look at alcohol and tobacco advertising in magazines and consider how these work. What methods of persuasion are being used? Who are they aimed at? How effective are they?

▲ It's important to control the
drug and not let the drug
control you.

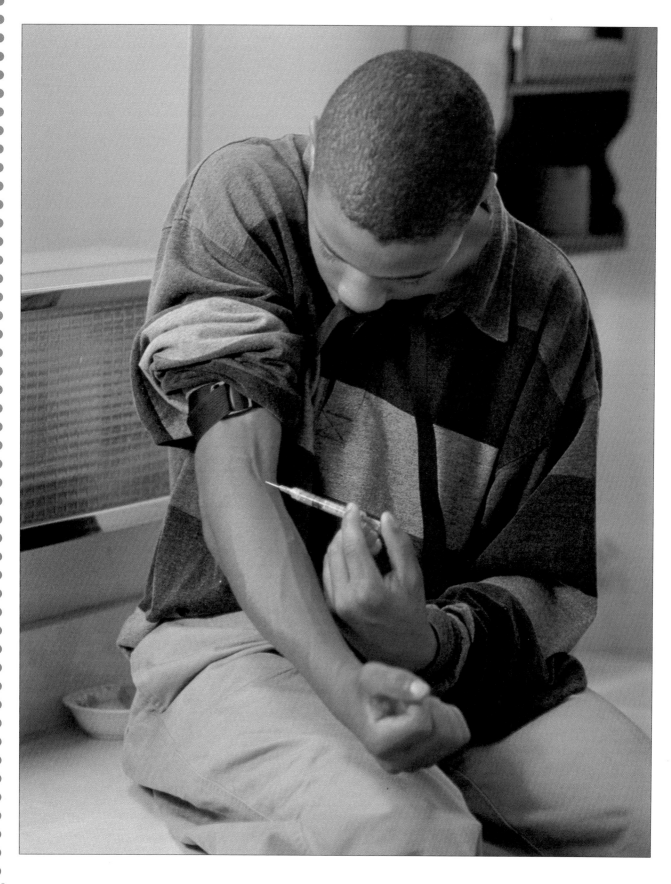

When do drugs become a problem?

How do you know if you have a problem with drugs? As far as alcohol's concerned, if you feel that you need a drink several times a day, or if you find that you simply can't do something without having a drink first, then you have a problem. Exactly the same goes for tobacco. If you need alcohol and tobacco to prop your life up, even though it might not be bothering you now, you are at a level which will seriously damage your health. Drinking more than 50 units of alcohol per week for men and 35 units for women is definitely dangerous, while smoking at any level will cause damage. As for illegal drugs it's impossible to say what levels and amounts are dangerous, partly because the drugs themselves are made illegally and so vary enormously in strength, and partly because we don't really know that much about them. Clearly, though, injecting a 'hard' drug such as heroin is more dangerous than, say, smoking it. Injecting is more likely to lead to dependence because high doses are more likely, the 'rush' is more sudden (and you may need to increase doses to get the rush), and the injection ritual itself may become very important.

Leaving all the amounts aside, though, if your drug use is dominating your life and you're not happy with the amount that you're using and finding it difficult to stop or reduce it, then you have a problem.

Drug addiction, alcoholism and dependency on cigarettes

Addiction means that someone is so dependent on a drug that serious harm is being done. This dependence can be physical,

◀ Injecting a drug is more dangerous than smoking it.

▶ If a drug is starting to control your life, then you have a problem.

where you need to keep taking the drug to avoid physically unpleasant withdrawal symptoms, or it can be psychological, or mental, where you need the stimulation, pleasure or escape from reality which the drug gives you. Psychological dependence can in fact be more difficult to break than physical dependence.

Many, but not all, of the illegal drugs can lead to dependency of one sort or another. Amphetamines, cocaine, heroin, barbiturates and tranquillizers can all lead to mental dependency, and physical dependency, too, is possible with heroin, barbiturates and tranquillizers. It's also quite easy to get mentally dependent on alcohol and tobacco, and both of these drugs can lead to physical dependence. Apart from the short- and long-term health damage that dependency on any of these drugs may cause, dependence tends to mean that you have to increase the dose to get the same effect, or even that you have to keep on taking a drug just to stay 'normal'. At this point you don't even get any pleasure out of the drug any more – which is maybe why you took it in the first place. It's not really known whether solvents, Ecstasy, LSD or cannabis can actually lead to dependency of either sort, but it's worth remembering that if you feel that you can't relax without smoking a joint, or you can't face the day without having a go at your mum's hairspray, then you need to ask yourself if you're still in control.

▼ **Having the support of other people can help reduce drug dependence.**

Reducing your dependence on these drugs is difficult but it is possible once you've made the decision, and once you've got the support of other people, whether they're professionals or your family or friends.

Ruining your life

The trouble with drugs is that using them can have an effect on your life for years to come, either because of dependence and all the problems that it causes, or because of the short- and long-term health effects that using the drug can have.

Injecting drugs is the least common way of using drugs, but it's the most dangerous for a number of reasons. If you share needles, you run the risk of contracting the AIDS virus HIV as well as other infections such as hepatitis. Even if you don't share needles, injecting can be dangerous if you accidentally

▲ **Getting hold of enough of the drug to stay 'normal' can create more problems.**

inject into an artery instead of a vein. This can cause gangrene which may mean losing a finger, toe or even a limb. You can also damage yourself badly when you inject because street drugs do not always dissolve properly, and small bits of undissolved tablets or powder can collect under the skin and cause painful abscesses. If these are not treated, they can lead to blood poisoning and serious illness. Accidental overdose is more likely if you inject because all the drug enters the blood stream at once – if the drug is unusually pure or you have miscalculated, the amount you inject may be more powerful than your body is used to, and the consequences can be fatal. Usually, street drugs are mixed with something else like sugar or laxatives, or possibly cheaper drugs in order to make them go further. Sometimes, however, they may be mixed with toxic substances like bleach, which are extremely dangerous.

Apart from the health problems which go with drug use, drugs can affect your life in ways that hang on even after you've stopped. Ex-alcoholics, for instance, are rarely able to enjoy a drink every now and again. Like ex-smokers who dare not have even one cigarette, previous alcoholics cannot risk a drink because they may become dependent again. Being dependent on drugs can mean that your drug use comes to dominate your life, and your major concern will be getting hold of your next dose, or finding the money to buy it. For most young people, the main danger with using drugs is the fact that most

of them are illegal and there will always be a possibility of arrest and criminal proceedings, along with a damaging criminal record. For some, the whole thing will get even more serious, and they may become involved in an adult criminal lifestyle which may stay with them for life. If it's out of control, drug use can also mean that you become generally apathetic and not particularly bothered about where you're going and what you're going to do next. This may mean that you miss opportunities at school, college or work that you may not have again.

Effects on families and friends

If your drug use becomes a problem for you, it's very likely that it will be a problem for your family and friends as well. Apart from the worry it may cause them, you could end up hurting them without meaning to. Many of the side effects of long-term drug use – moodiness, irritability, forgetfulness, depression, anxiety, feeling persecuted and

general bad physical and mental health – can all make you pretty difficult to live with. You may even hurt someone physically if you become aggressive and violent during a drinking bout, for instance. If you are pregnant and you take drugs, you could damage your baby or even lose it altogether – a baby's body is far less able to cope than an adult's. If you use drugs which can cause physical dependence, your baby could be born suffering from withdrawal.

If your relationship with your parents is already under pressure, your drug use may well be the last straw. You may also be making unreasonable demands on your friends in expecting them to stand by you, put up with your moods, and possibly protect you from discovery. Your parents and friends will find it difficult to know where to begin to help you, especially if you won't let them, or if you won't admit you have a problem.

Group work activity

At a party you are offered a drug you don't want to take. As a single individual, how do you manage to say 'No' in the face of a number of others who want you to join in? One of them is your best friend and one is someone you're hoping to go out with. Role play the situation.

▲ If you have a problem with drugs, your family and friends may be affected, too.

Authority figures

Parents are quite likely to have fixed ideas about smoking, alcohol and drugs. If you are experimenting with drugs and your parents realize what is going on, they may put a lot of pressure on you to stop or tell them more than you want to about you and your friends. Their reactions may really annoy you, but try to remember that they are probably worried or feeling guilty – a lot of parents feel very responsible for their children and think they must have failed as parents if their children leave the 'straight and narrow'. Don't forget, too, that many parents will have come from a generation or background with no experience of illegal drugs and will have far less information than you about it all. What information they do have may just be a collection of frightening statistics about how many people have died while using Ecstasy or how LSD makes people jump out of windows.

One of the major problems for young people in this situation is that adult attitudes seem very hypocritical – your parents may smoke and drink regularly and yet go off at the deep end when you do, or when you use a drug which you consider is less harmful than tobacco or alcohol. There's no easy answer to this – you may be right – but this shouldn't influence what you do and the decisions you make. Don't fall into the trap of using drugs just to annoy them or make a point.

What you should do, though, is talk to your parents as much as possible and let them see that you are responsible and well-informed and that you can be trusted to look after yourself and stay in control. Part of the difficulty for them will be accepting that you are growing up and don't need looking after so much any more. You certainly won't convince them of this by clamming up and cutting them out of your life – they'll simply get more anxious. You could also try letting your parents meet your friends. This will make them feel more in touch with your life and, hopefully, less worried about what you are doing.

► **If you try to keep a dialogue going with your parents, they may understand more and be less worried.**

The law on drugs, smoking and alcohol

The laws on the use of drugs, alcohol and tobacco and on their possession and supply are often confusing, contradictory and inconsistent, but you should know what they are, and also what will happen if you are found breaking the law.

Legal drugs

Alcohol

The law on alcohol depends very much on what age you are. If you are under fourteen, you cannot go into a pub or a bar which sells alcohol, unless you are with an adult and the landlord says it is OK. In any event, it is against the law to drink alcohol in a public place at this age. It is not illegal for young people between five and sixteen to drink alcohol in a private home.

If you are over fourteen and under eighteen, you are allowed to go into a pub but it is illegal to buy alcohol, or to drink it, even if someone else buys it for you. A landlord has the right to tell you to go.

If you are over sixteen and under eighteen, you can buy beer, cider or wine if you are drinking it with a meal. Otherwise, if you are under eighteen, you are breaking the law if you buy alcohol from pubs, shops or off-licences.

◄ **Drinking and driving carry very heavy penalties and can even mean a prison sentence.**

If someone driving is stopped and found to be 'over the limit', they are breaking the law, and will automatically lose their licence. As a rough guide, a woman who drinks more than four units or a man who drinks more than five units will be over the limit. Remember, though, that the effect of alcohol varies from person to person, and that being under the limit does not mean that anyone is safe to drive. Even if a person has been drinking less than these amounts they are ten times more likely to have an accident than if they haven't been drinking at all. Again, if someone is on foot and is judged by the police to be 'drunk and disorderly', they can be picked up and charged.

Cigarettes
There are no laws about smoking if you are in private: you can smoke at any age. If you are under sixteen and you smoke in public, a police officer can take your cigarettes away.

◄ In this situation both people are breaking the law.

▼ If you are taken to a police station, make sure you know exactly why you are there.

If you are aged ten to fifteen, you can be taken to court for trying to buy tobacco in any form for your own use. It's also illegal for a shopkeeper to sell tobacco, cigarettes or cigarette papers to someone under sixteen for their own use. Once you're sixteen, you can legally buy and smoke tobacco in public.

Glue sniffing and other solvents
There are no laws against sniffing glue or other solvents, but the police can pick you up and take you to the police station if they think you are a danger to yourself. This is not the same as arresting you, and if you decide to leave, they can't keep you there unless

they do arrest you, in which case they should make it clear why.

It is illegal to sell solvents to someone who is under eighteen. Buying solvents for someone under eighteen is also illegal.

Illegal drugs
The law on illegal drugs can be confusing: tranquillizers, barbiturates or even heroin can be legally prescribed by a doctor, but their possession, use and supply in any other situation is, generally speaking, illegal. That said, it is not illegal to pick and eat magic mushrooms raw, but the drug psilocybin ,which they contain, is illegal, and you can be

charged for preparing mushrooms by cooking, brewing or drying them. Again, it is not illegal to possess Valium, but it *is* illegal to supply it.

Possession

Having a drug on you and personal use of illegal drugs are seen as the same offence. Possession can include more than one person: if you are sharing a joint with someone else, you are both guilty of possession and passing a joint around a group of friends is possession too. You can also be charged with 'past possession' if you admit to having had a drug in the past, even if you do not have any on you at the time that you are stopped by the police.

Supply

Selling or dealing in drugs is treated as serious and can land you with a heavy fine or prison sentence. Supply doesn't just cover major dealing in drugs for profit – by law you can be charged if you give someone a small lump of cannabis as a present, for example. It's worth bearing in mind that if you're picked up by the police for possession – you can make things worse by saying someone gave it to you (which gets *them* into trouble for supplying), or if you say that you bought it for someone else (which gets *you* into trouble for supplying). You

can be guilty of supply even though you haven't made any money out of the deal. It is also illegal to grow cannabis plants or to let someone else use your home to do this or make and sell other illegal drugs.

If you are picked up by the police and they find any drugs on you, you can be charged and may have to go to court. If you are under eighteen, you will probably be fined, and you will now have a criminal record. The size of the fine or sentence, if you get one, will depend on the type of drug involved, your age, and the type of offence you are convicted of. Don't forget, too, that taking illegal drugs from one country to another is very serious and in some countries carries a death penalty or at least long imprisonment.

Group work activity
You are cleaning up your teenage daughter's/son's bedroom when you discover some unidentified pills. Extremely anxious, you confront her/him and demand to know what is going on. How do you feel? What do you say? Role play the situation.

▶ **If you are charged, you may go to a Magistrate's Court.**

Who can help?

The first person who can help you is you yourself. Once you've decided that you need to stop smoking or cut down on alcohol or other drugs, you're on your way. This is because you will be taking responsibility for yourself and making decisions for yourself, rather than letting others make them for you. Taking responsibility for your own actions, instead of blaming other people or the drug you are using, is one way of keeping or regaining control.

Feeling positive about yourself
You also need to believe in yourself and your future. Many people coming off drugs really concentrate on the things they've always wanted to do, like learning carpentry or writing, or on sorting out their lives in terms of housing and training schemes. In more general terms, you need to think about the effect of your drug use on the things you want out of life, both now and later on. If you smoke twenty cigarettes a day, are you really going to be any good as a footballer, and are you going to be able to afford that round-the-world trip when you're older? How and why you stop will be up to you. You may get sponsored to stop, or you may decide to stop because it is

▲ Freedom from any addiction gives you the energy and confidence to try other things.

◄ You are more likely to succeed in giving something up if you make the decision to do so yourself.

unpleasant for other people. Whichever reason you choose for stopping, you will experience a positive feeling about yourself and your life. You can save the money you would have spent on cigarettes to buy something you've always wanted, you notice smells and tastes more, you can learn new skills or take up a new hobby to keep yourself occupied.

Help from family and friends
The best help that family and friends can give you is their support, whether you're still using drugs or whether you've made the decision to cut down or stop. You can only get their help by talking honestly to them about what you're doing and why, and keeping on talking. If you're thinking of going to a drug

agency, it may be a good idea to ask other members of your family to go with you, either for support or because it may be easier to explain to them how you feel if a counsellor or other outsider is there. If problems with your family are at the root of why you use drugs in the first place, you might feel that talking to them is out of the question at first. If you go to a drug agency or other service for support, you may feel able to tackle problems with your family later on when you're more in control.

What services are available to help?

Smoking

Your doctor, health centre or pharmacist can help you and give you advice on giving up smoking. Health Education units also give free information and advice and sometimes run Stop Smoking groups. The telephone number will be in the directory under your health authority. There are also helplines you can ring for advice, counselling and details of your nearest Stop Smoking group. The numbers are at the end of this book.

Drinking

There are a number of specialist groups which can help with problem drinking, both for those who drink and for their families. They offer information, advice and

self-help groups. Some are especially aimed at young people and all of them are completely confidential. Their addresses and telephone numbers are at the end of this book.

Illegal drugs and alcohol abuse

The first step is to find out what services are available in your area. They are all listed in a booklet called *Drug Problems: Where to get help,* which is kept by Citizens' Advice Bureaux and libraries. The booklet is produced by SCODA (The Standing Conference on Drug Abuse), who will also send you a list of services in your area if you phone them. Their address and number is at the end of this book along with other regional numbers.

Advice, information and counselling services

Specialist services can help you decide what to do and support you while you do it. You can talk your problems over and find ways of dealing with them, and discuss practical things like housing, work, finding new friends and so on. Many work with local doctors so you can get medical help if you need it. They can also refer you to a hospital treatment centre if necessary.

◀ **New friends can give you new confidence.**

If there is no specialist service in your area, a social worker from your local authority Social Services or Social Work department may be able to help. Youth workers can also help. General counselling services are also available and you can get details from the addresses at the end of this book.

The National Health Service

You can also visit a specialist hospital treatment centre if you have a letter from your GP, probation officer, social worker or drug counselling service. You will either be treated as an out-patient, or you may be admitted to hospital if you are finding it difficult to stop using drugs while still at home. Your doctor is not allowed to tell anyone – including the police, your family, your school or your employer – that you are a drug user. If you are addicted to opiates, your doctor must fill in a form about you, but personal information about you on the form is not available to anyone else unless they are a doctor.

Rehabilitation houses

People who have particularly bad problems with drugs might live in a rehabilitation house for up to a year while they learn to cope without drugs. Social workers, doctors, probation officers and drug counsellors will help you to apply.

▼ **A rehabilitation house, away from family and friends, may be the best place to adjust back into normal life.**

Self-help and Community Groups

The main idea with self-help groups is that all the people involved have similar experiences and can support each other because of this. Groups hold regular meetings with the aim of helping people come off drugs and stay off them for good. So although you may join a group in the first place because you need help, you may find eventually that you're helping yourself by helping others.

▲ **Counselling sessions and self help groups help people to help themselves – and each other.**

Helping agencies and organizations

Drug Services

SCODA
(The Standing Conference on
Drug Abuse)
Waterbridge House
32-36 Loman Street
London SE1 OEE
Tel: 071 928 9500

Freephone Drug Problems
Ask the operator for this and you
will hear a recorded message
giving a telephone contact
number for every English county.

Scottish Drugs Forum
266 Clyde Street
Glasgow G1 4JH
Tel: 041 221 1175

All Wales Drugsline
1 Neville Street
Canton
Cardiff CF1 8LP
Tel: 0222 383313
Free Helpline: 0800 220794

Northern Ireland Council for
Voluntary Action
127 Ormeau Road
Belfast BT7 1SH
Tel: 0232 321224

HIV infection and AIDS

SCODA and Scottish Drugs
Forum can provide information
(see above).

The National AIDS Helpline
Tel: 0800 576 123
This is free and confidential and
gives local advice.

Alcohol Services

Alcohol Concern
305 Gray's Inn Road
London WC1X 8QF
Tel: 071 833 3471
Information, advice and access to
over 40 local centres.

Alcohol Concern Wales
Brunel House
2 Fitzallan Road
Cardiff CF2 1EB
Tel: 0222 48800

Scottish Council on Alcohol
137-145 Sauchiehall Street
Glasgow G2 3EW
Tel: 041 333 9677

Northern Ireland Council
on Alcohol
40 Elmwood Avenue
Belfast BT9 6AZ
Tel: 0232 664434

AA (Alcoholics Anonymous)
PO Box 1
Stonebow House
Stonebow
York YO1 2NJ
Tel: 0904 644026

AA can put you in touch with a
local group:

London Region Helpline:
071 352 3001

Scotland Region Helpline:
041 221 9027

Northern Ireland Region Helpline:
0232 681084

Wales, South-West Region:
0222 373939

Wales, West Region Helpline:
09945 282

Advice and Counselling

NAYPCAS
(The National Association of
Young People's Counselling and
Advisory Services)
17-23 Albion Street
Leicester LE1 6GD
Tel: 0533 558763

NAYPCAS can put you in touch
with a local youth counselling
service, usually for people under
21. You need to enclose a
stamped, addressed envelope.

BAC (British Association for
Counselling)
37A Sheep Street
Rugby
Warwickshire CV21 3BX
Tel: 0788 78328

BAC can refer you to a counsellor
in your area. Some services are
free.

Information about solvents

Re-Solv (The Society for the
Prevention of Solvent and Volatile
Substance Abuse)
30A High Street
Stone
Staffordshire ST15 8AW
Tel: 0785 817885

Re-Solv is a charity which
publishes leaflets, booklets and
videos, and which can put you in
touch with local helping agencies.

Information and Help for Smokers

Quitline
England: 071 487 3000
Scotland: 0800 848484
Northern Ireland: 0232 663281
Wales: 0222 641888

Quitline can give you advice,
counselling and details of your
nearest Stop Smoking group.
They will send you an information
'Quitpack' if you ask.

Self-Help Groups

Narcotics Anonymous
UK Service Office
PO Box 1980
London N19 3LS
Tel: 071 351 6794

NA can tell you where the nearest
meeting is held or help you to
start your own self-help group for
people with drugs problems.

Help with Legal Problems

Release
388 Old Street
London EC1N 9LT
Tel: 071 729 5255

Release can give you advice on
legal problems arising from drug
use. Outside normal working
hours and at weekends, there is
an emergency number: 071 603
6854

Further reading

Many of the organizations listed on the last two pages produce leaflets on various aspects of drug and alcohol use. The following three organizations also produce leaflets on a range of topics.

TACADE
1 Hulme Place
The Crescent
Salford M5 4QA
Tel: 061 745 8925

Health Education Authority
Hamilton House
Mabledon Place
London WC1H 9TX
Tel: 071 631 0930

Institute for the Study of Drug Dependence (ISDD)
Waterbridge House
32-36 Loman Street
London SE1 0EE
Tel: 071 928 1211

Reading for parents and families:

Drugs and Your Child,
(1992, ISDD)

How to Help: A Practical Guide for the Friends and Relatives of Drug Users
The Blenheim Project
(1988, ISDD)

Parents: What You Need to Know about Solvent Sniffing
by Richard Ives.
(1990, ISDD)

Teenagers and Drugs
by John Davies and Niall Coggans
(1991, TSA Publishing Ltd)
A tape and booklet advice and information pack for parents

Teenagers and Alcohol
by John Coleman and Coralie Tiffin
(1993, TSA Publishing Ltd)

For Drug Users:

How to Stop: A Do-It-Yourself Guide to Opiate Withdrawal
The Blenheim Project
(1988, ISDD)

What Works? Safer Injecting Guide
Exeter Drugs Project
(1990, ISDD)

Changing Gear: A Book for Women Who Use Drugs Illegally In Britain
The Blenheim Project
(1988, ISDD)

Coming Off Tranquillisers
by Shirley Trickett
(1991, ISDD)

D Mag
(ISDD)
A magazine for recreational drug users aged 16 plus

Tomorrow I'll Be Different: The Effective Way to Stop Drinking
by C. Beauchamp, with an introduction by Elton John
(1993, Viking)

Drunk In Charge of a Body
Brook Advisory Centre
(1991, Brook Education and Publications Unit)
Tel: 071 708 1390

Let's Discuss Drinking
by R. Armitage
(1987, Wayland Publishers Ltd)

Glossary

Abscess A collection of pus or poison in a cavity; an infected boil.

Abuse To make bad use of; to use something wrongly; to use a drug for purposes other than medical ones.

Addiction When someone is so dependent on a drug that serious harm is being done.

AIDS Acquired Immune Deficiency Syndrome, which develops in people who have contracted HIV.

Bronchitis Inflammation of the lining of the bronchial tubes.

Cirrhosis Wasting away of an organ such as the liver.

Gangrene Death of part of the body.

Hepatitis Inflammation of the liver.

HIV Human Immuno-deficiency Virus, the virus which can develop into AIDS. It is passed through blood to blood contact or through sexual intercourse. Sharing needles increases the chance of becoming infected.

Opiate A drug containing opium.

Paranoia A chronic mental state where someone suffers from delusions of grandeur or persecution.

Physical dependence When the body gets used to a drug and the person has to keep taking it to stop withdrawal symptoms.

Psychological dependence When a person thinks they need to carry on using drugs to cope with life.

Rush The start of the effects of a drug after it has been taken/injected.

Tolerance When increasing amounts of the drug are needed.

Withdrawal When the body reacts to the drug being stopped.

Index